DAUGHTER

OF THE

BOTTLE

Orange Rose Press

ISBN: Paperback: 979-8-9885364-4-4

Photography by Omar William David Williams via Pexels/Canva
Cover Design by Amber Campbell

DAUGHTER
OF THE
BOTTLE

Amber Campbell

ORANGE
ROSE
PRESS

Other titles by Amber Campbell

The Ones

Missed Arrows: Poems

For the readers on the cliff's edge.
It's okay to love through tears.

Table of Contents

IN YOUTH

Don't look under the rug

Picture frames decorate my home
With smiling faces and frosting-covered lips,
With children laughing and summer eclipses,
But don't look in the corner.
Where I grew up,
Fathers drank and mothers smoked,
But you aren't supposed to remember that.
You aren't supposed to see it memorialized
In their final photo before goodbye.
My home is clean and pristine,
And the cobwebs in the corner are
From the change in seasons
And not mirages meant to scare you.
The floors are sturdy like good wood should be,
But don't look under the rug!
No, it's clean, that's why you shouldn't look.

The little girl you see inside
May be shattered in mind, but her body is alive,
And if she looks pretty and smart and quiet,
That's all that matters. Wouldn't you agree?
Isn't that what you love about me?

A Daughter's Love

Riley ducked her head under the wooden awning of the apartment building and into the shade. She unlocked the door at the top of the stairs and stepped inside, dropping her backpack on the floor beside a small pile of dusty shoes. The kitchen and living room reeked of Hamburger Helper, cheap whiskey, and cigarettes, even though she'd asked him not to smoke inside.

Riley took a deep breath and exhaled through her nose, her eyes focusing on the trail he left behind. She took the bag out of the trash can and tossed out the red plastic cups filled with butts. Finding two cups half-full, Riley poured the warm Kentucky Deluxe down the sink. She emptied the overflowing ash tray and tied the garbage bag.

Returning outside, Riley kept her eyes low toward the dumpster behind the building. She knew no one could smell the shame she carried, but because the smells permanently glued themselves to her nostril hairs, she couldn't mask the fear that etched on her face when her downstairs neighbor had seen the collection of bottles in their thin, white trash bags and offered the sickly-sweet note of prayers for her and her troubled father.

After that, Riley checked the calendar each time she took a trash bag out to ensure the downstairs busybody would be away each time she dumped another collection of grief and regret. Riley tossed the bag into the rust-colored dumpster, shielded her eyes once more from the harsh afternoon sun, and bounded up the stairs two at a time.

Opening the kitchen and living room windows, Riley lit a cinnamon candle and set it on the linoleum counter. She grabbed a dry washcloth and moved to straighten the photos on the bookshelf just across from her father's favorite recliner, lifting the ones of her mom and dusting them off. In the oldest family photo they had, she and her sister Robyn wore matching pink and white dresses while their mother sat them on each knee, her dyed blonde hair woven in curls that draped her face. Their father stood behind them, his shoulders rigid but a crooked smile on his face. He wore a suit with a pink tie to match. Riley shook her head, remembering how tense her father's hand had felt on her shoulder as he struggled to find the pose the photographer so desperately wanted for their portrait. In the end, her father gritted his teeth and barked that the next picture would be the one they chose so he could go home and get out of the uncomfortable suit.

Fortunately for him, the next picture was the one her mother loved.

Riley dusted the portrait and set down the frame next to a signed Mike Buck football from the Saints' win against the Browns in the only NFL game her father had ever attended. She turned the glass box so it faced the living room, careful to avoid the nick in the glass from when her mother threw it at the table. Riley picked up her backpack on her way to her bedroom, closed the door behind her, and turned on the lights.

Various shades of blue decorated the small room, from the custom, floral paint design on the walls she and Robyn did the year before Robyn left for college to the blue, white, and black geometric-style comforter thrown atop her bed. Riley took out her economics textbook as the front door opened.

She raced to the end of the hallway as her father walked inside, beaming as he kicked off his shoes. Sweat soaked his tattered uniform, and she reminded herself to buy more detergent.

"Hey!" she said, walking into the light.

"Hey, kiddo," he said, giving her a one-armed hug as he walked into the kitchen. He pulled a glass from the counter and opened the freezer.

Riley took a seat on one of the two chairs at the table. "How was work?"

"Sucked. I had to fix close to twenty machines today." He poured a glass of bourbon and tucked the nearly full bottle in between the frozen pizzas and meals in the freezer.

"I take it Dennis had to fix the same numbers?" Riley asked.

Her father chuckled. "Yeah right, I think he fixed seven." He walked over to the table to sit down across from her. "How was school?"

"It was good. I got an 83 on my English test."

"Good job! Did you put it on the fridge?"

"Dad, I'm seventeen. I don't put stuff on the fridge."

He raised his eyebrows and pointed to the hallway. "Go to your room and get the test. I'm putting it up right now. Go, go."

Riley smiled as she rolled her eyes and hurried to her room. She flipped through her English folder, leafing through papers until she found the test, and took it back to the kitchen. She held the exam out to him on her palms. Her father took it from her and stuck magnets on the top and the bottom. "That looks nice, don't you think?" he asked, standing back.

"It looks great, Dad. I'm going to see if I can finish reading this chapter before my eyeballs fall out," she said, walking backwards out of the kitchen.

"Don't study too hard!" he said. Riley chuckled in response. She left her door open as she began reading for her econ assignment.

The light from her window cast a purple and pink hue in the room as the sun set, the opened blinds shadowing the wall behind her bed. Just as Riley finished reading, she turned on her lamp. Her eyes shifted to the picture of her and her dad that sat on the nightstand. She pulled her hands together and wished she knew how to pray. Her hot breath hovered in the air and floated through the gaps between her fingers and onto her palms. She wiped her hands on her pants and closed the textbook, picking it up and packing it in her backpack. She changed into sweatpants and one of her mother's old shirts and shuffled into the living room.

Her father sat in the recliner. The light from the kitchen shined into the living room, but only enough to see his silhouette and the outline of his disheveled hair. The rest of his body disappeared with the dark. No trace of smoke reached her nose, but she noted the empty liquor bottle sitting on the kitchen counter.

"Dad?"

He looked up. She could see him turn his head and smile as he faced the light. "Hi, coyote. Done studying?"

"Yeah," Riley choked out, rattled by the old nickname. Robyn had always been bird, but since she couldn't pronounce Rs as a child, Riley had been called Wiley, resulting in the obnoxious Looney Toons reference she only heard when her father was feeling sentimental. "What 'cha doing?"

"Sitting," he said. He held up his empty glass. "I was drinking, but it's gone now." He lowered the glass to the arm of the chair and stared into a dark corner of the apartment. "It's all gone now." She could hear his voice crack and dug her fingernails into her palm.

"What's gone, Dad?" she asked. Riley stepped forward but kept her arms near her body, her fingers knotting together painfully as she forced the other emotions at bay. She swallowed. She swore the sound echoed in the apartment, but she knew it was the blood in her ears.

"Everything."

"I'm here."

He looked toward her, his smile lessening, wrinkles covering his forehead. Wrinkles she didn't remember being there. "You are. I love you."

"I love you, too, Dad."

She watched his gaze go past her to the bookshelf. She could see the family portrait out of the corner of her eye. Her arms trembled, his previous breakdowns flashing through her mind. She had to steady herself, to be strong for him. She tucked a loose strand of hair behind her ear, but it fell back when she lowered her gaze to the floor. The half-moons in her skin burned, but she kept her nails embedded where they were.

"I'm a terrible father," he said, his eyes never leaving the picture on the shelf.

"No, you're not," she whispered, but it sounded more like a croak. "We just need to work on your husband skills." He tried but couldn't fake a chuckle, the sound resonating from his throat reminding Riley of a choke. He looked down at the glass in his hand and set it down on the dinner tray table beside the armrest. Her muscles ached from flexing, but at least then she knew that she was shaking because of fatigue and nothing else. Her dry mouth failed to produce a semblance of comforting words, but the silence ended sooner than she expected.

"It's getting late. Why don't you head to bed?" he asked, sitting up in the chair and kicking down the footrest.

Riley swallowed again. "Are you sure? We can watch *Whose Line* for a little while until you fall asleep."

She watched him shake his head. "No, go on to bed."

Riley turned away and somehow her legs shuffled her away from the living room and to the edge of the hallway. She rested her hand on the wall. "Good night, Dad."

"Good night, coyote. Sleep tight." She waited and watched him close his eyes and lean against the back of the recliner. She broke her gaze and followed the hallway to her bedroom. She closed the door and slumped onto her bed. Sitting down, she was eye level with the picture of her and her dad from her fourteenth birthday party. Both of their eyes were closed from laughing so hard, and a tear had fallen from Riley's eye as she had fought to catch her breath.

Her mother had taken that picture while Robyn sat on the floor, covering her mouth to hide her snort. A few months later her mother left after her father cheated the third time with the woman who lived two buildings over, the same woman who swore she was friends with Riley's mom. Robyn left for college the following fall and when she returned for her first semester break, she stayed with their mom.

Riley didn't agree with what her father had done. She tried to get him to slow down the drinking, for the sake of his health and bank account, but she knew none of that mattered so long as their family was broken up. At least the family was together before despite the emotional strain and turmoil they suffered during the fighting. Riley could wake up and check on her sister and parents sleeping in the beds they were supposed to be in.

Now, with the family divided, she had to drive to the other side of town to see her mom, and when Robyn didn't visit over her first break following the split, Riley didn't know whether her sister knew how harshly that affected their father and his drinking or if she even cared. Even though she missed them, Riley had no choice but to stay.

Her mother couldn't forgive him for being a horrible husband, but Riley couldn't hate him for being the best dad she'd ever known.

Fears

Don't forget to mind your fears
Because they haven't forgotten you.
Remember their names
Because they still whisper yours.
Can therapy fix the damage created
From a person who bled out
And spread their sadness onto the floor
And into the mind of a child?
Can therapy fix the broken person
Even as the news outlets and the government
Tell us no one is broken?
How can I recover when no one knew
Of the fractured mind and splintered heart?
How does one put together a soul
When it was formed from shards of love?
How do I let go of the fear
That has constantly comforted me
From the demons it sparks?

2003

Sawyer stacked the pillows on a swivel chair from the kitchen table and climbed toward the top shelf of the closet. He stepped on the door handle for additional stabilization, but the pillows shifted under his footing. Pouting, he slid off the pillows and onto the chair and straightened out the mess. He could see his prize, The Game of Life, resting just a few feet above his head. He stalked the door to his sister's room, but when he didn't spot her at her desk, he stole the pillows off her bed and dashed back to his room. He constructed his ladder and stood back in awe of the seven-pillow tower. He gripped the back of the chair and stepped onto the seat with his right foot.

"Sawyer!" his sister barked. He jumped, lost his balance, and fell onto the floor. He rubbed his butt as she marched toward him. "What are you doing? You could get hurt! Come on, get up." She yanked him to his feet, her eyes narrowed, but she checked him out anyway. "Don't do it again, or I'm telling Mom."

"But I wanna play Life," he whined, pointing to the board game in the closet. She followed his finger, rolled her eyes, and turned around. "Come on, Abby! Play with me."

"I don't want to play. I have chores to do," she said. Sawyer ran after her, watching Abigail navigate over the three dogs sleeping on the living room floor and return to the pile of laundry on the table. He slumped down beside their German shepherd, Angel. She didn't acknowledge him as he scratched her ears, but the golden retriever puppy jumped up and ran to him for attention. She proceeded to lick his hands until she wiggled close enough to slobber over his cheeks.

"No, Sammy! That's gross!" He giggled, pushing the puppy away. Sawyer watched his sister fold one of his shirts. "No, Mom always hangs that one up!" He ran over to her and took the red shirt from her hands. Sammy followed in suit, sliding across the slick linoleum tiles in the kitchen. Abby waited as he struggled to straighten the shirt across the hanger before leaving it on the hanging rack on the outside of their parents' bedroom.

"Why don't you just take it to your room now?" Abby asked. She grabbed a towel. At the sound of her voice, her miniature schnauzer left his spot beside the entertainment center and nestled himself in the dog bed under the kitchen table.

"I'll do it later," Sawyer said. He strolled over to the island, tapping his fingers on the edge before grabbing spoons from the drawer and drumming a tune. He stopped only after Abby threatened to tell Mom if he didn't. "I'm bored. Will you play a game with me?"

She finished the laundry after spraying the bottom of a pair of jean shorts with water and folding them. "Why don't you play a video game?" she asked.

"It's no fun alone. Let's play Life! You can be the blue car," he said, poking the stack of his sister's clothes on the corner of the island with one of the spoons. "I'll be the red one."

"I thought green was your favorite color."

"I'm too old for green. I'm red now. Vroom!" Sawyer took off toward his room. The sudden movement sparked Sammy to chase after him. Abby looked over the laundry on the table, straightened out her mom's pile, and squatted to eye level with her dog. She stroked his head until he opened his eyes.

"Come on, Dot. We said we'd call Brittany after we finished the chores," she said, standing up and grabbing the house phone off the desk in the living room. The schnauzer trotted after her down the hall until she stopped at her brother's room.

Abby crossed her arms and leaned in the doorframe like she watched her mother do every time Sawyer misbehaved. She straightened out her back but couldn't point her right foot across her left without losing her balance. She tucked her hair behind her ear and raised her eyebrow.

Sawyer looked up from his tower. "What are you doing?"

"I'm being Mom," she said, sticking out her lips.

"Why are your eyes so big? Mom's eyes aren't that big."

"They are when she's like this!" Abby reinforced her lips and raised her eyebrows higher, throwing her hands on her hips. She leaned forward to emphasize the action, but it resulted in losing her balance again and swaying to the side. Sawyer stepped back, bumping into the closet door.

"You look like that clown we saw at trick-or-treating," he said. He shuddered but climbed back onto the chair. Abby dropped her act and peered into the closet.

"You're going to get hurt, and I'm going to get in trouble."

"I won't get hurt. I know what I'm doing. I'm already seven, you know."

"That's what you say every time before *I* get in trouble. Now come down." Abby held out her hand, tapping her foot. Sawyer reached for the box, but the pillows shifted, and he sunk to the seat of the chair. His shoulders fell in disappointment, and Abby stepped onto the chair. She reached past him but couldn't grab the box. Sawyer wrapped his arms around her waist and tried to lift her. She lifted her heels off the chair and stretched her arms and fingers until she could touch the edge of the box.

Pushing the rest of the stack of games toward the wall, Abby yanked on the Game of Life as Sawyer pulled her back onto the chair. Abby clutched the box to herself as Sawyer swung in tandem with the creaky chair. They stayed frozen until the chair stopped moving. When Abby deemed it safe enough to move, they climbed down from the chair.

"Want to play at the kitchen table?" Sawyer asked, throwing the pillows on his bed.

"No, I don't want to play, and make sure you put my pillows back in my room. Poor Dot didn't have a pillow to sleep on last night because someone took it," she said, handing him the game.

The front door slammed open against the wall, and they heard their mom's footsteps first. The dogs barked in unison, dashing out of the room. Abby stepped toward the hallway when the front door slammed closed, and she stopped mid-step.

"I don't care!" their mom snapped, and the kids heard her keys clank against a kitchen countertop.

"Then why do I care?" their dad bellowed. Sawyer sat down on the floor, shaking as he grabbed his green striped tiger off the bed. Abby ushered Sammy back into the room before closing the door silently. The shouts rose in volume, but the walls muffled the words until they were incomprehensible. Sawyer grabbed Sammy and cradled her in his lap. She licked his hand twice before laying down her head on his knee.

Abby picked up the game and set it down on the floor, pushing away his dirty clothes. She didn't need to bite her tongue when she thought about the laundry she believed was finished in the other end of the house. She pulled out the game board and held out the red car to Sawyer.

"Here's your car," she said.

He took the car, leaned over to plop it on the college side of the board, and picked Sammy up to move her over his other leg. She fell limp, licking his hands as he tried to lift her, and he giggled until the shouting increased. All three of them froze. Abby looked around the room until she spotted the radio and turned the dial to 103.2, their favorite station. She turned the volume as high as she could without the music seeping into the other areas of the house. They caught N*SYNC in the middle of the chorus for "It's Gonna Be Me," but neither sang along with the familiar lyrics.

"Here's your person," she said, placing the blue peg in the red car. She proceeded to place a pink peg in her blue car and set down the piece on the college side as well.

"Look, they're the same! I'm red and blue, and you're blue and red," Sawyer said, pointing to the board.

Abby laughed over the music. "They are the same! That's cool." They spun the wheel as the incoherent shouting blended with the new single from Christina Aguilera. Sawyer dug his fingers into Sam's fur as he adjusted his body to lay his head on her back.

"Why do they fight?" he asked as Abby moved her car four spaces.

"I don't know."

"Will they fight when we go to Grandma's house?"

"No, they don't fight in front of other people." She grabbed some money from the bank and motioned for Sawyer to spin the wheel. He pushed his red car six spaces and Abby handed him a L.I.F.E. tile.

"So why do they fight in front of us?"

Abby's hand hovered over the wheel. She reeled her arm back in, grabbing a teddy bear off the bookshelf and brushing the hair out of his eyes. "I don't know."

Dear father,

I still love you.
I will always miss you.
But I don't miss the midnight screams
And turning up the radio to drown out
Your angry tantrums, and how I watched
My mother sweep glass off the floor
From a vase you hurled against the wall
Because you feared my brother growing sicker
And feared losing my mom because she might one day
Realize you're more flawed than you let her believe.
I raced off to college and couldn't sleep in my dorm
Because the quietness of my roommate spooked me,
So I played white noise in the black room
And watched my hair gray a few decades too soon.
My piercing blue eyes that attracted everyone
Only reminded me of how gray they could fade
If I followed down the path you chose.
In a way, perhaps I meandered too far off the trail
Because now I drown in words, aching for relief
From a pain so ingrained in my bones
That removing it might stop my heart
And suck the air from my lungs. The blended scent
Of musky cigarettes and outside air I still can't name
Haunts my dreams when I'm alone, and the home
I watched you grow ill and thin in
Flourishes in new coats of paint and cinnamon pinecones.
Perhaps there is no coming back from this,
And perhaps I will always fear men
With a drink in their hands,
Smoke billowing from the cigarette between their teeth,
And perspiration beading down their faces,
Because I know what men are capable of when they feel

As though they have nothing left to lose.
One day I might heal from the irrational fear that stops me
From enjoying a bar or staying out until the sunrise,
But years of therapy and three specialists later,
And I still tremble at the sight of glossy eyes,
Wisps of a phantom haunting me from the grave
Like they did when you were alive.

IN LOVE

DNA Mutations

I hate that I have your temper
But my mother's tears
Because I cry when I want to scream,
And no one takes me seriously.

Generational Trauma Impasse

Condensation rolls over my fingers,
Their tips frozen to the glass,
But the burning I should feel
Fades before it lasts.
The whiskey never hits my belly
The way it hit yours.
The corn never ferments my soul
The way it seemed to cure yours.
The ice melted before I got the chance
To finish the remedy you swore
Bandaged all the broken pieces you wore.
Why don't I get the bliss of blackouts?
Why don't I get to scream and yell
And blame the liquor I forced into my mouth?
Why don't I wake up forgetting
The atrocities committed against my loved ones
And pretend like everything is golden?

You wanted me to be better than you,
So I bottle my anger like your whiskey
And swallow my illness like I do my pills
Because I can only be as sweet
As my trauma allows me to be.

Blackout

When you blackout, do you dream?
Do you enter a hellscape of your worst mistakes?
Do you see the faces of those who fought back
But didn't survive the backlash?
Or is there no sense of space and time,
Only a dark, endless expanse of an abyss?
A silent void where even dust can't thrive,
And you're imprisoned within its echoing binds?
Or is it the only time you feel happy
Because you finally feel nothing?

Blameless

My therapist said it's not your fault you drink and that something happened long ago that caused severe anxiety and depression and possible PTSD, and that's really why you drink.

My therapist said that medication wasn't acceptable in the 70s and 80s when you were a child, so maybe your parents passed on their problems to you without meaning to.

My therapist said that only recently did society accept mental illness as something that requires additional help and prescriptions, and not just a lobotomy and electrical shocks.

My therapist said you need help just like I'm getting help, but that your generation didn't believe in therapy because it was like admitting you're broken, and Gen Xers aren't broken.

My therapist said I can't blame you for being a byproduct of your depression and anxiety because it started before you knew how to fight back.

But my therapist said not to blame myself because I did nothing wrong, and to act in a way that protects my boundaries and physical and emotional safety when you lose control.

My therapist says things like these are *blameless* because there's not a singular moment of decision where someone says, "I want to be an alcoholic."

So now I see my therapist and so does all my generation and the ones after mine because they can't blame their parents for the emotional abuse, physical abuse, sexual abuse, and financial abuse they experienced, but our parents and grandparents can call us selfish and spoiled and privileged snowflakes because we seek understanding and help instead of substances to numb the pain.

I don't blame you, but how do victims seek retribution when their inflictors have done unintentional harm? The drunk driver is sentenced to prison for vehicular manslaughter, but the parent maintains custody when throwing plates across the house and punching holes in the wall.

If there is no one to blame, why are there victims?

Sempiternal

I hate that when I'm lost on the road, I call you.
I hate that when I'm sad, you cheer me up
With video games and candy.
I hate that when I know you're in the wrong,
I will never turn my back or call you out
Or demand an apology for your behavior
Because I'm scared of angering you
When this whole time you were scared
Of terrifying me.

2013

Sawyer lugged the black suitcase into the corner of the living room as his older sister, Abigail, struggled walking past the dogs to get into the house. Sam limped over to her, sniffing her clothes and bathing her hands in saliva. Shadow, the rambunctious husky, leaped over Sam to get closer to Abigail as Dot whined from the couch.

"Down girls! Let me get in!" Abigail laughed, wrapping her arm around the husky's neck as she jumped up. Sawyer whistled, holding out his hands for the husky and keeping her back until Abigail closed the door and found a seat on the couch. Sawyer released Shadow, and soon all three dogs were suffocating Abigail as she pet Dot and Shadow with her hands and Sam with her foot.

"Do you want to keep this in the living room for now?" Sawyer asked, patting the suitcase.

"Okay, down Shadow, down. Good girl. Yeah, it's fine for now. Not that I have a room to put it in anyway," she said, picking up the schnauzer and cradling him in her arms. She nestled her nose in his cheek.

"That's what happens when you move out and leave me," Sawyer said, grabbing two glasses from the kitchen cabinet.

Abigail looked around the living room as he poured the sweet tea. The sofas were moved in accordance with Shadow's kennel, placed in the corner between the secondhand sofa and loveseat. Sam nudged Abigail's suitcase as she curled into a large blonde ball on the dingy carpet. A zipper brushed against her head as she closed her eyes.

Shadow jumped around, her tail slapping Sawyer so hard he nearly lost the drinks.

"Jeez, dog! Relax a minute." He handed Abigail a glass and set his tea down on the coffee table. He picked up a chewed tennis ball and tossed it toward the master bedroom. Shadow took off, kicking up the rug in the kitchen on her way.

"She's so big," Abigail said as she took a sip. Shadow brought back the deformed toy and ran back to the room. Sawyer threw it again.

"She'll be three in February. Hey, isn't that how many years you've been gone?" He smiled as she reached over to slap his arm.

"I've been back in between semesters. Besides, it's not like I can just jump in a car and drive 400 miles to see you every weekend."

"Speaking of driving," Sawyer said, reaching into his pocket and pulling out his wallet, "guess who's license came in the mail last week?"

Abigail squealed, clapping her hands together. Dot jumped in reaction and dug his nose deeper into the sofa cushion as he tightened the curl of his body. "No way! Let me see, let me see!" She ripped the card from his hands, tilting the sides to see all the imprints. "Look at my baby brother, all grown up! You're so cute!"

"It's not cute. Kelly said I looked sophisticated and handsome." He sat up, straightening an invisible collar and holding up his chin with his hand.

"You're super cute!" Abigail said, tousling his short hair before throwing back his card.

"I'm too old for cute. Men aren't cute. We're tough and sexy."

Abigail laughed, leaning back against the sofa. She kicked her legs up and pulled them in as she giggled into her knees. Sawyer shoved her, forcing her to let go of her shins to catch herself before she fell off the couch. He stood up, picked up the tennis ball, and tossed it in the direction of the hallway.

Shadow stopped mid leap and ran. Abigail scratched the sleeping schnauzer's ears as he laid on her feet.

"I told this guy at school his name was Dotcom, and he laughed," Sawyer said, taking a seat in the recliner.

"Did you tell him how old he was?" Abigail asked, her fingers outlining the bones of Dot's cheeks. The schnauzer blinked, and she could see the cataracts covering the majority of both his eyes.

"No, I didn't think it would make a difference."

"It does! He's fourteen. He was born when the internet was."

Sawyer slapped his thighs, and Shadow jumped into his lap. "I think the internet was around before the 90s."

"Close enough. When are mom and dad getting back?" she asked.

"They should be here eventually. They said they wanted to pick up some food for a party Mark is having tonight."

Abigail leaned her head against the sofa. "They're going out the first night I'm back?"

Shadow settled in his lap and panted drool on his jeans. Sawyer scooted over so that her tongue hung over the arm rest. "Looks like it. Want to go out and get dinner? I can drive legally now." He twisted his upper body to see Abigail around his husky. He grinned, his eyebrows dancing the worm.

"I'm not getting in the car with you. I don't trust the state's judgment." She laughed, ducking and covering Dot as a pillow flew their way. "I want to stay inside. I feel like I've been going out every night this past month. Is there anything we can do here?"

Sawyer motioned to the door, and Shadow jumped down. He let her outside and waited to see if the others would follow, but Dot stayed beside Abigail and Sam snored. He closed the screen door. "You lived here for eighteen years and you're asking if there's anything to do?"

"I feel like I haven't even been here in forever. I don't even know where anything is."

Sawyer pointed toward the refrigerator. "The kitchen is directly in front of you, and you're currently in the living room. To your left you'll find the hallway leading to my bedroom and the bathroom."

"You're hilarious," she chuckled. "What games do you have?"

"Which games are you talking about?"

Abigail leaned into the sofa. "Let's be old school. Which board games has Mom not thrown away yet?"

"Want to see? I think all the ones we still have are somewhere in my room." Sawyer hustled down the hallway. Abigail reached the bedroom door as Sawyer picked up a pile of clothes and tossed them to the center of the floor.

"That's disgusting. How do you still have clothes to wear?" she asked as she climbed over the mess.

"I wear things twice. I save water cause I'm green like that," he said as he moved boxes aside on the top shelf of the closet.

"That's not green, or maybe it is, how long have these towels been here? I think this might be mold growing." Abigail picked up a shoe and poked a towel on the carpet. She shuddered, dropped the shoe, and stood in front of the open closet. "What games are up there?"

Sawyer pulled down a garbage bag of winter coats and dropped them on the floor. "I see Monopoly, Connect Four, Cranium, Yahtzee, and Battleship, I think." He pulled out the stack of games and juggled them on his forearms as Abigail stood on her toes to see past his tall frame.

"I see Life!" Abigail shouted, pulling on her brother's arms until Sawyer tripped on the pile of jackets and fell onto the floor, catching himself but dropping the board games and scattering the pieces across the carpet. He sat up, glaring at Abigail as she climbed on top of the dresser at the end of his twin bed and leaned into the closet to grab the board game. Shadow galloped into the room and barked at Sawyer until he shooed her away. He stood up and nudged Abigail's legs, but as soon as she trembled and leaned sideways, he reached out and grabbed her waist, keeping her upright. Abigail reached for the board game and yanked it off the top shelf as Sawyer pushed her backwards. She fell onto the bed, Life clutched in her hands. She grinned, holding out the game. "Want to play?" she asked.

"That sounds reasonable," Sawyer said, kicking the other games and their pieces against the wall. "Just as you threaten to kill me, you offer to play Life."

Abigail smirked, jumping off the bed and running into her old bedroom. Sawyer yelled after her, complaining about the mess on his floor. "There was a mess long before I got there!" Abigail shouted. She set the board game down on the only clear part of the floor and moved the cardboard boxes of their mom's things to the side, blocking most of the dressers. The tinge musk mixed with dog dander and faded cigarettes itched her nose. She grabbed a perfume spray off her desk, some scent her mom recently fell in love with at Bath and Body Works called Carried Away, and sprayed every inch around her. She set down the bottle next to a stack of fake bills as Shadow barreled in, jumping up to greet her and sneezing twice, shaking her head so violently her white fur flew into the air.

Sawyer coughed as he entered the room and managed to pull out two white dog hairs from his mouth. He knelt on the floor, still grimacing, and whistled for Shadow to join him. All three dogs ran. Shadow jumped on Sawyer's leg, forcing him to double over, before leaping over his head to get to the bed. Sam limped down the hall and collapsed beside Sawyer on the floor. Dotcom tripped over both Sam and Sawyer to reach Abigail as she shuffled through the pieces.

"Which color car would you like?" Abigail asked. "We have blue, red, white, and yellow. I'm blue!"

"What happened to the green car? That was always my car," Sawyer said, making a mess with the hotel pieces as he searched for his piece.

Abigail stopped placing her peg in her car in mid-action. "You always wanted the red car."

Sawyer shook his head. "Green was my favorite color. I think I'd remember my favorite color, duh." He put down the top of the box and picked up the red car, grumbling under his breath and pulling the car away from Shadow as she peered over his shoulder to sniff it.

Abigail handed him a blue peg person and placed her car on the career space. Sawyer drove his red car to the college space and picked up the career cards. "Hey, look! I'm red with blue, and you're blue with red! That's awesome!" he said as he shuffled. Abigail dropped her face in her hands, running her fingers through her hair as he held out the cards. Just as Abigail reached for the middle card, two doors slammed from outside. Shadow jumped off the bed as she sprinted for the front door, her tail wagging so fast that she slapped Sawyer's face on her way out. Sam struggled to stand and follow her lead, her tail swaying.

"I thought you said the parentals wouldn't be home until later," Abigail said, mulling over her three choices.

Sawyer shrugged and rubbed more hair off his face. "They weren't supposed to be. Maybe they forgot something. Want to go see them?"

"Of course, but I want to surprise them," Abigail said, smiling. "I want to see how long it takes them to realize I'm back after they see the suitcase in the living room."

"Alright, which career do you want? I know you got the police officer and the teacher, but what else did you get?"

Abigail opened her mouth when the front door opened and slammed against the hallway wall. She looked up at Sawyer, and he rose to his feet before she blinked. He peered down the hallway as their father entered, yelling at the dogs to get back as he slammed the door shut. Sawyer jumped behind the door frame, waiting until he felt the footsteps of his father fade before closing his sister's bedroom door. He sat down on the floor by the time the yelling reached the siblings' end of the mobile home, but the words were incoherent. When Sawyer heard tidbits of the argument about the money and the party, he took out his phone and started playing music. He set the phone down and turned the volume as high as it would go.

Abigail picked up two of her cards and dropped them on top of the blue stack. "I picked the entertainer."

Sawyer nodded and picked up the green stack without shuffling them. "You can only pick the red or purple salaries. And then we can spin for turns."

Abigail grabbed the middle card when another door slammed, and she jumped and dropped the card. Sawyer picked it up off the board. They heard the bellowing voice of their father walking out of the house. The high-pitched voice of their mother followed, and the front door opened again. Abigail pulled her dog closer to her.

"They didn't even come and see me," she whispered. Sawyer looked up, and Abigail could feel him watching her, but she refused to cry in front of him, distracting herself with the card she chose that rested in his hand. Sawyer leaned over the board to give her the card.

"They'll come by," he said. "This is a good salary. You should take it."

"It's not red or purple," she said.

"Pretend you're Taylor Swift," said Sawyer, grinning and putting down the stack of cards. Abigail smiled and set down the yellow-coded $100,000 salary card beside her career card, tossing her hair like her favorite singer. Sawyer rubbed his hands together. "Now, let's spin to see who goes first. Do you still want to play?" he asked. His hands froze midair, waiting.

Abigail blinked, swallowing as she nodded. "Of course. We have to play. We always play Life together."

Sawyer nodded, pointing to the wheel. "Ladies spin first," he said. "Maybe this will be the game where we finally win."

Abigail forced a smile, spinning the wheel as hard as she could.

Men are offended when I fear them
Instead of asking
Who first made me afraid.

- Not all men

Better Than

When I finally marry, it will be with a man
Who holds my hand when we stroll the supermarket
And kisses the top of my head watching a sunset
And overuses 'I love you' until I never forget.
He will be patient, strong, and level-headed,
And I won't fear his temper when I mistake
Something large for something small
Because he will understand I'm human
Like everyone else around us.
I will find a man better than
The one who drinks too much
And smokes too much
And yells too much
And hugs too much
And laughs too much
And causes a rush in my head
As my heart wrestles with
How much bad is too much
To outweigh the good.

Borrowed Stories

My first car was a faded blue Honda.
I don't remember the model anymore.
I drove it for only a couple years in high school
Before I left for university out of state.
I learned to drive in it,
And to this day, I can drive without the passenger mirror
Because for two years, my car didn't have one
After you hit a mailbox coming home late at night.
You had driven home buzzed from the dive bar
Where you swore you'd been alone,
But the heated whispers that followed me the next day
Told me more than you'd ever say.
Those mirrors ended up saving my life
When I'd saved enough money to buy a new car
And narrowly caught sight of the candy apple red Mustang
Zooming past me on the highway.
Why I bothered looking, I'll never know,
Since I never had a reason to look before,
But it was probably your slurred voice in my head,
Giving me life lessons after I'd been in bed for hours,
Advising me not to switch lanes when I catch sight
Of a crow flying past the windshield
Like the farmer's almanac of drunk adages.
But perhaps there's truth to your madness
Because I saw the crow, looked in that shiny new side mirror,
And veered to the right as soon as I saw the flash of red.

Toothpaste

Bridget wiped down the counter with a clean washcloth that was once a vibrant green that had dulled to a puke shade of yellow-green-white after years of product and bleach. With a final stripe across the countertops, Bridget stepped back to survey her work. Chips were properly sealed, canned goods were placed in the cabinets, and the remaining flowers from her work anniversary bouquet from her supervisor had wilted and found themselves in the compost outside in the flower beds.

She rinsed off the flower vase and left it to dry. The sun of an early afternoon pierced through the window, lighting up the sink in a glow of yellow. Collecting her cleaning supplies, Bridget turned up the volume on her instrumental jazz music and moved the cleaning into the bathroom.

She picked up a band aid wrapper and tossed it in the trash. The sun rays glinting through the thin window above the shower caught on something shiny, and Bridget looked again to find the remnants of a beer bottle.

She hadn't intended to drink last night, and with each wipe of the mirror, she pleaded with her brain to let it go. But the sun continued to hit the bottle until she huffed, kicked the trash bin to the side, and flinched as the bottle rattled against the force. It didn't break, something that hadn't crossed her mind, and Bridget bit her cheek until it bled. Her mind never thought of useful ideas, only embarrassing moments to remind her of how little she had progressed despite her boyfriend repeating how well she was doing.

The mirror would have squeaked if she applied any more pressure, so she grabbed the disinfectant to spray down the sink. Bridget never intended to drink, but she was at least conscious of when she started drinking. She never drank to get drunk, but with such a low tolerance, two hard ciders was all it took for her speech to slur and her cheeks to flush and her balance to forget how to cooperate with gravity. Before the second bottle emptied, Bridget had sang along to half of Ed Sheeran's newest album and picked up the cat to waltz through the living room. Granted, her version of the waltz was a two-step with three added steps, but she danced and spun and kissed poor Meatball's face every few seconds. When she noticed the room spinning even when she stopped, she carried Meatball to his favorite cat bed and kissed him a few more times before he curled into a ball and ignored her praise.

"I think you danced him to sleep," her boyfriend said, a hint of a smile to his tone. Bridget wrapped her arms around him and kissed his cheek. "Or maybe your breath knocked him out."

Bridget recoiled, but Logan grabbed her wrists and held her in place.

"That wasn't a dig," he said, and this time, he locked eyes with her as best he could while hers flitted from his eyes to his lips. "It was a joke."

"I know," Bridget said. But she never really knew. She always assumed she was in the wrong. If she wasn't, no harm done. If she was, she had an advantageous start to fixing whatever it was. Logan was the first man she dated to call her out on it and relate it to her childhood trauma, but she refused to fix something that wasn't broken.

Logan sighed and eased his grip on her wrists. "Do you mind if I play some music? You can still dance to it. Heavy metal is actually the easiest music to dance to."

Bridget smiled, hoped she smiled. "Yeah, go for it. I'm going to lie down for a bit."

"Come on, I wasn't trying to start anything," Logan said. This time he turned around on the couch and took his eyes off the laptop screen. "You can keep drinking."

Bridget nodded. "I still have an open bottle," she finally responded. She turned around and tripped over a pile of junk: an extra keyboard, a couple shirts, a cardboard box of knick knacks that she intended to put on the shelving that still sat in its box underneath the box of knick knacks.

"Careful!" Logan reached out to catch her, but the refrigerator beat him to it. Bridget trembled where she stood, but her fingers gripped the fridge's edges until she knew both her feet were flat on the ground. "Are you okay?" he asked.

"Yeah, yeah, I'm okay."

"We need to clean that this weekend."

Bridget nodded. "We will."

"TLC called yesterday and wants to add us to their line-up on the next season of hoarders." He chuckled and took a drink of his sweet tea.

Bridget willed her lips into a smile as her eyes drilled holes into the ground beneath her. "Yeah, I'll get to it. Saturday I don't have any plans."

She wasn't sure if Logan responded before or after he restarted his movie, but she strolled down the hall with a wave in her step, using the walls to keep her upright. She had an open bottle, but it was in the freezer, and she wouldn't be going back for it now. He'd seen her stumble despite being nowhere near the legal limit, but it didn't matter. One fuck-up was all it took for someone who had already been to rehab twice in the last six years.

Bridget stood in the doorway of their bedroom, the dresser across from the bed overfilling with more of her things that she needed but didn't yet have a home for. Following the glow of the hallway light and leaving the bedroom light off, she gathered the layer of clothes and shifted them to the bed. She wouldn't sleep with them on it, not this time. The rest of the cluster were, thankfully, things she could organize without bothering Logan, although she was surprisingly much more sober now than she had been a minute ago.

Nothing like former demons waking up to kill a buzz.

A wake of sleep overtook her, and she hurried to put away the folded clothes before they wrinkled. She'd clean first thing in the morning, while he was still asleep, which is where she found herself shortly after sunrise. After an hour the kitchen and living room had been cleaned and organized, to the best of her abilities without getting out a drill and putting up the shelves like she said she'd do last month, and only the bathroom remained. The island catch-all had yielded a few bathroom items she needed to finish the job after wiping down the mirror and cabinets, and lastly was the goodie bag from her dental appointment.

She tossed out the baggie immediately and tucked away the toothbrush and floss in a lower drawer for when they needed them. The toothpaste, however, was always needed since they relied on the free miniature toothpastes to save money. Before Bridget set it down, her fingers trembled, and she twisted off the cap and peeled off the seal. Now she could set it down. She watched the seal slip from her fingers into the trash can and willed unsuccessfully for her trembling to stop.

The reflection in the mirror changed as though on cue, and instead of her vibrant natural brown hair, she saw the brighter shade of strawberry-blonde her ex-boyfriend had insisted on. Bridget stepped back, and the coldness of the wall seared her skin with flashbacks. Trey was the sweetest guy she'd ever met, let alone dated: always held the door, brought her food, and complimented her each time they hung out with friends. But the niceness faded as soon as the eyes looked away, and if he wasn't drinking to justify his actions, Bridget was drinking to beat him to the numbness.

A loud clap woke Bridget up, and she jumped out of bed, the comforter twisting around her legs as her arms grappled for the nearby dresser. Before her eyes opened, the brightness of the bathroom light hit her face and she turned away as the rancid odor of morning breath hit her from the side.

"Haven't I told you to open stuff when you put it up?" Trey demanded.

"Yes." Bridget opened her eyes but squinted the more she faced the light.

"Then why wasn't this opened?" He held something up to her, and Bridget strained to focus on the tube in his hand.

"I don't know, I must have–"

"Forgot, sure." Trey stomped back to the bathroom, opening the door wider until the light spilled into the bedroom and lit everything up in a yellow, fluorescent haze that somehow made Bridget's sight worse. "It's not that hard to do."

"I didn't say it was," Bridget said before her brain could wake up and scream at her to shut up, let him vent, and go back to bed. But if her brain was asleep, her anger was awake.

"They why don't you do it?" he screamed. The shift in tone shocked Bridget, and she turned back to the bed. She raised her knee to climb up when a hand gripped her elbow and she gasped. "What are you doing? If I have to be awake, so do you."

Bridget froze. She didn't cry, not anymore, not when it only made things worse. Only he was allowed to cry after he'd had too much to drink and realized how cruel he was, but it still ended in Bridget not doing enough, not being enough, not supporting him enough. Just when she thought she had a grasp, Trey proved again how he always held the upper hand.

"You do this shit on purpose to get back at me!"

"No, I–"

"Shut up! I'm talking, not you."

Bridget kept her eyes opened, focused on the light switch on the wall until Trey proceeded to brush his teeth and pause in his tirade. Worthless. Hateful. Depressed. She was everything wrong with humanity, and he could leave at any moment if only he didn't love her so damn much.

"Great, now I'm going to be late," he spat. She watched him wipe his mouth and flinched when he waved his hand in the air. "Go back to bed. Why are you still up? You have the opening shift, don't you?"

"Yes," Bridget whispered. She climbed into bed and dove into the covers. No one ever warns children that the monsters evolved to find the body beneath the blankets, but it made her feel safer every time.

"I'll be home later. Love you," he said.

"Love you, too," Bridget replied. She waited until the door closed and the truck started and the seconds turned to minutes before she cried. She would remember the toothpaste next time. He wouldn't have been late if he hadn't woken her up, but now he ensured he'd never be late.

Meatball slunk between Bridget's legs, and she blinked away the reverie. Her brunette waves framed her face in the mirror, and she held her breath until she saw Logan's face in the bed behind her. She stood by the bed, unmoving, trembling, and pet Meatball without realizing he was meowing so loudly. Logan rustled, and suddenly Bridget's brain jolted into action and she scooped the cat into her arms and into the living room. But before she grabbed his toy, she checked all the mini toothpastes in the drawer and unsealed them all.

Her therapist and Logan told her she didn't have to live in survival mode anymore, but Bridget knew better. She knew she was trained correctly, because a woman who fears her partner is one who will always outlive the woman who fights for her worth. Regardless of who she ended her life with, she would end her life at nature's hands and not his. Never his.

My lover never asks if I ate that day.
My lover inquires what I ate
When I divulge the ache in my belly
Stops me from returning to my dreams.
My lover ponders the meat from midday,
If perhaps it was on its last leg,
Or if the fibrous vegetables met
With the cheese in my stomach
And built an impasse in my intestines.
I nod in the dark. Surely one of those.
Because the musk of rum and Coke
On the pillow next to mine
Could never be the cause of my sorrows.

Addicted to Addicts

My throat burns as the drink hits it.
I sought a partner to care for
While never trusting them with me
And not believing anyone could protect
A woman when she's drunk because I saw
What happened when she closed her eyes.

I'm as sick as my former partners, but instead
Of seeking a shot, I seek them. I find
Fulfillment in enabling the weak because
I was raised to fetch beers and cigarettes
And could twist off a bottle cap between
The insides of my thumb and index finger
Before I entered middle school.

They can't help themselves, and neither
Can I. I was taught how to nurse a drunk,
Care for the depressed, and calm
The anxious without addressing the haunted
Look behind my eyes when I finally
Closed the door and hid in my closet.

Hi, my name is ______. I'm addicted to addicts.
This is my first meeting, and I can only stay clean
So long as I'm tucked away,
A hermit to the metroplex of busy bodies
And exhaust fumes. But tell me you can't sleep
Without a drink, that you only partake recreationally,
And I will find your truth, and I will become your cure.

Even though we both know the disease
Is what you brought you to me.

A Woman's Purpose

I'm a broken person without a person to fix.
Your vices give me purpose.
I was taught that a woman's place
Is in healing and dependency,
But you'll never heal
Until you're dependent on me.

Molotov Cocktail

I should have known a man who gets high with me
Wouldn't be a man to rise high with me.
I knew you'd never take a bullet for me,
But I never imagined you'd take a bullet to flee from me.
You tasted the lead on her lips
And the arsenic between her hips,
Left me with a poisoned kiss,
And bit the bullet between her teeth,
Believing she could heal you better than me.
My anguish lapped at your bitter remnants,
And I only felt love when she touched you.
I wondered if I tasted like her
As you licked my tongue as if searching for the flavor
That only she alone could muster.
I laid alone in your bed,
Thoughts of her touching you in my head.
Even though I was never one to wed
A man who loved another, I vowed
To never ruin another like you ruined her.
Had her believing you would change,
Had her believing you loved her
When you only loved the title you bestowed upon her
When you left her with a child.
How could you call me and reminisce,
Lying to me about remembering happier times
With your new wife beside you on the couch
That you once worshipped me on?

Aesthetically pleasing ailments

My, my, darling, this just won't do.
Brushed hair, ironed clothes, no make-up to do?
How will anyone on the streets
See you and not immediately think
You're suffering from a physical disease?
Addiction is a mental affliction, yes, I've heard,
But it doesn't have to be the only one, sweet girl.
Come, step inside, and for the smallest sum,
I'll make you the belle of the sanitorium.
More cheekbones, more rib bones, more clavicle,
Too much meat, you still look healthy.
How can society feel terrible for your fate
When you appear that you've recently ate?
Addicts don't eat, dear, they only consume.
Your ailment isn't believable unless you run on fumes.
Embrace your life, these drabs aren't a costume.
In fact, everyone will be envious of your pale hue.
How dare tuberculosis steal the title of consumption
When users for centuries wasted away to addiction?
And how embarrassing for a disease
That can't steal lives without being chosen, like me.

Honey

I tried to discover the secret formula
To stay in the warmth of that honeyed moon,
The sweetness and the light,
But it eluded me when I brushed against it.
I dream of tasting the sugar on my tongue
Like my lungs devour oxygen
And burn under the rays of the night sun,
But grasping it is like catching smoke.
Is it all me?
Am I clinging to falsehoods and gray realities,
Willing you to be the fantasy in my head
Instead of the ache in my chest?
I need more affection than you provide.
I am shamed when I taste honey
That didn't drip from your lips,
And I drown beneath the waves in my mind,
Basking under the moonlight I once touched
That's now mere redness under my skin.

Collision

You hit me like a freight train,
Colliding into me, stealing my breath,
Calming my racing heart and giving me rest
From those who treated love like a contest.
You filled my cup so full I can't contain
The joy exuding from my lips,
Blocking out pain to teach me healing,
And I loved you before you helped me forget
That everyone I love loses their breath
When I steal their air and finally let them rest.

Chosen Victims

Love is no more than an idea
With all the neglect we feed it.
Love is staying with the one who yells
Because it means they care enough to fight.
Love is supporting an addict
Because it shows how much we value them.
Love is forgiving a cheater
Because it reminds the world we're ride or die.
But what if we let ourselves die?
What if we fell
        and kept
           falling
              until we
                couldn't feel
                  rock bottom?
We choose to love the ones who have known
How to love unconditionally
Because we were raised to believe that love
Does not exist without pain and fear.
Love is the willingness to lay down our arms
And embrace others so tightly they no longer question
If they will ever feel tenderness before the swift kiss
Of death calls them to a forever home
Where we may not find them again.
We choose to love victims
Because we refuse to call ourselves victims,
But the day we do is the day we rise
And finally create love that does more than survive.

Abusive Love is a Magic 8 Ball

I don't need a therapist to tell me
That I seek men who drink
Because it's all I know.
I don't need a therapist to diagnose me
With codependency, emotional trauma,
Anxiety, and mild depression.
I don't need a therapist to listen
To the problems swimming in my head
Before I've even touched the pillow.
I need a phantom of every father
Who ever drank to hide from his problems
To wrap me in a hug and say sorry.
Yes, I blame you. I always did,
But I don't know if I will tomorrow.
Ask me then. Ask me when I've cooled off
And calmed down and don't hold my knees
To my chest on the ground where I learned to cry
Without making a sound. Ask me tomorrow, and I'll
Answer truthfully. And if you don't like
The response, ask again later.

Nine-Dart Out

I met you in the bar where you said you left her.
I drove miles and nights to spend mornings in your arms,
And I mistook your cheeky lines for charm.
I gave you everything I had,
But you shoved me away, saying I must have gone bad.
You let me believe I was flawed for not being fun.
You said we'd be better in the next life,
But there's no second chance for tripe.

Nine darts to win with a hat trick,
And you somehow won on a digital board with a steel tip.

Faded Summer

The orange hue of a faded summer
Transforms the rickety bench by the water
Into a kaleidoscope of sweaty hands and tanned leather
That smells of your '09 Nissan beater
Where we kissed during bright weather
And did more waiting for storms to get better.
I can taste the shift to autumn
As crisp as I licked your lips of your roommate's rum
That you stole when you caught him
Stealing your cash, but that crash at rock bottom
Is the only reason you didn't run
When I told you where I'd come from.
Winter brings the chill in my bones
When I realized I was finally alone
Because you stopped blowing up my phone,
And I hated how I missed when I didn't know
How quickly I'd grow to love you so.
A flowery scent of geranium and jasmine,
A pop of yellow and purple and mint,
A spring of life floods my senses
While I accept that life is about building fences
To shield my peace and not to keep out sin.
The seasons change, but your bottle stays the same.
How long until you forget my name?
How long until I forget the pain?
How long until we wash the stain
Of pale ale and doomed dreams down the drain?

When does enabling
Become surviving?

Am I truly free of addiction
If my daily habits to survive
So I can live the life
I dreamt of as a child
Prevent me from rising
Because thriving entails forfeiting the
Lip biting, leg shaking, and hair twisting?
I can say no to drink, pills, and smoke,
But the carnal urge to pick my skin
Makes me believe this genetic mutation
Still found its way in.

Illness

Sickness takes until there is no more to steal.
Illness consumes until the belly pops.
I sought understanding in empty vessels and brown bottles
When all I needed was to stop. Breathe.
I watched the man who taught me everything
Waste away to a measly 140 pounds,
Half the man you are in the photos on our wall.
I held your hands when you cried,
I fetched heating pads and medicine,
And I withheld tears so you wouldn't know how sad
It truly felt to realize the terror that shook me at night
Wasn't a man with a bourbon buzz
But the fear of losing the comfort of
An imperfect but unconditional love.
I chased others to find an acceptance I never found again
Because each night I held your hand as you fell asleep
Only reminded me of how many never comforted me
When they'd finally had their fill of drink.
There's a difference between addicts
And those suffering from addiction,
And I never realized it until I'd met the former
To realize the latter was always our relationship's affliction.

IN DEATH

We collected the bag of ashes from the funeral home.
Mom and I thought they'd given us Belize sand
Because the movies always make the dead look
More like fire pit ashes instead of the assortment of tans
You came out in. We laughed when we used a funnel
To pour the ashes into a Crown bottle
Because you loved your whiskey,
But I shrieked when some fell and hit my thumb,
And I asked mom what I should do
If the ashes that landed on me were from your penis.
She stopped pouring as her body shook with laughter.
My aunt said my humor was terrible, and it is,
Because had you been with us,
You would have said the joke before I did.
But then mom laughed and said
There probably wouldn't be any ashes for that
Because there wasn't enough of one to make ashes,
And we paused the whole whiskey-bottle-urn business
Before we spilled you all over the laundry room
For us to walk through for the next twenty years,
Wondering which pieces of you
Would have stuck between our toes
And which pieces would have sunk into the floorboards
To haunt the next family that resided in it.

Playing with Fire

When I dream, I forget you're dead,
And I see you again
And hold conversations with you,
But that's only when there's enough medication
Coursing through my blue veins
To put me deep enough into REM
To speak to you without remembering
You're gone.
If a Benadryl mixed with melatonin lets me hold
A conversation with you again,
What would happen if I mixed them
With a pint of Guinness?
A shot of whiskey?
A green-laced gummy?
Would I smell the stale cigarettes
And outdoor scent I never learned to name?
Could I awake and believe you're next door on the porch,
Listening to the birds and throwing the ball for the dogs?
Is it stupid of me to try to mix these things just for a glimpse
Of seeing your face before the cancer took your body
And left us with only a skeleton to tend?
Does it make me an addict to want the same poison
That took your liver and almost your life,
To see you again when I won't remember the dream
A few hours after the sleep leaves my brain,
And I walk through the empty house
And past the broken-in and broken-down recliner
Where you lived your final year?
Is an addict someone who needs the fix
Because their body is dependent,
Or can an addict be someone who uses the results
To touch what was once real?

You always told me not to do the stupid ones,
Like meth, heroin, and crack,
But a little alcohol, a little marijuana, a little sleep aid,
And you can tell me in person,
As close to in person as a ghost can be,
To tell me this, too, is stupid,
And that I can't seek your advice
Because anything you tell me in my dreams
Are the things I already know and tell myself in your image
Because I would never listen to myself.
How ironic
Because I never listened to your advice before,
Before I understood why you drank,
Before I understood the anger-masked regret,
Before I understood no one knows the best answer
Because the best answer means there's a right answer,
And there's nothing right about living without hurting others
If it means we hurt ourselves in return.
But I sip my beer, the one you said I chewed,
And shit on the piss beer you drank,
And I watch the sunset instead of the midnight sky.
Perhaps that's the difference between an addict
And someone who misses an addict.

Cancer

Fuck you.

2023

The sunlight glinted through the dusty blinds onto the dirty floor, remnants of dog paws and footprints lit up in a personal spotlight. Abigail pulled her hair back for the fourth time and cursed the curtain bangs her best friend convinced her would look stunning on her. She was right: her face was framed in a more mature way that better reflected her 30s, but just as Abigail had assumed, their constant falling unleashed a rage inside of her she hadn't felt since junior high with her straight bangs when they'd grown out not two weeks after cutting them.

She was not a woman equipped to feel hair on her face if she was cleaning or exercising.

Securing the ponytail and the dozen or so bobby pins buried across her hair, Abigail returned to the dishes, scrubbing the last burnt remains of her mom's lasagna that didn't taste the same with fat free margarine and ground turkey as it did with salted butter and Italian sausage. She finally freed the last bit of stuck cheese when the front door flung open and slammed against the wall. Abigail jumped and splashed water across the counter.

"Celeste!"

"Sorry!"

Abigail chuckled and shut off the water as her niece enveloped her legs in a hug.

"Hey, Celeste, that was quite an entrance," she said. She leaned over and scooped up the small girl in her arms, soapy hands and everything, and planted a kiss on her cheek.

"I told her she has to enter the house like a human being," her brother said behind them. Sawyer set down a couple small, purple bags and a McDonald's bag that Abigail was sure had 2 uneaten nuggets and not a fry in sight. "We're still working on the human being part."

"Aunt Abby, can we play a game?" Celeste asked.

"Sure. In fact, Grandma brought over a bunch of games from her house that she left in the guest room if you want to find something there."

Celeste gasped and squirmed out of her grasp. As soon as her feet hit the floor, she bounded out of the kitchen and back into the apartment living room, speeding around the corner into the short hallway with three doors.

Sawyer sighed and his shoulders dropped as he sat down in one of the chairs.

"Everything good?" Abigail asked. She grabbed two mugs from the drying rack and started up the coffee machine.

"Yeah, just tired. She's got so much energy, and I don't want to stifle her, but damn is it a lot."

"I remember someone else being an equally endless ball of energy," Abigail said over her shoulder.

"Now you sound like mom," Sawyer muttered. "Thanks for watching her on short notice."

"It's no bother at all." Abigail sat down across from him and listened to the slow drip of the coffee. "How have things been with Isabel?"

Sawyer shrugged. "Same. She's being as cordial as she can be, but it's hardly an effort if you ask me."

"I get it. But I'm glad you're sticking with it."

"Finally?"

"You said it, not me."

Sawyer playfully threw a napkin at her, but it fell limply between them. "I heard it in your head. But you're right, and mom was right, and everybody was right."

"Not a matter of being right, kiddo, so much as doing what you need to do. And that woman is bad news." Abigail took a breath and listened for movement before speaking. "Is she still drinking?" she asked in a quieter voice.

Sawyer's smirk left Abigail's chest hollow. "Someone must be testing for her. She's even skinnier than last time, and a couple days ago, Celeste asked her why her eyes were yellow instead of brown like hers." He fidgeted with the keys attached to his belt loop. "How could I be stupid enough to be sober for my kid but give that same kid an alcoholic for a mother?"

Abigail reached out across the table, grasping at air as her brother huddled into himself. "It's not your fault she has a problem. You know that."

"I know the drinking isn't my fault, but choosing an alcoholic is." The drip of the coffee slowed, and Sawyer stood to pour drinks for himself and Abigail. He set down the blue mug in front of her and took a hesitant sip out of the green one. His eyes glanced over to the hutch in the corner of the kitchen before drilling holes into his coffee. Abigail already knew he was checking that the ashes were still in the urn, just like they did as kids, waiting for confirmation before speaking in case it was something they'd get in trouble for. "I wanted better for my kids."

"She already has better," Abigail whispered. Sawyer met her eyes with a small smile, but hurried to set down his cup as he heard the patter of tiny stomps barreling toward them.

"Can we play this?" Celeste asked. She held up a tattered, multi-colored box.

"You still have this?" Sawyer asked, gingerly taking the ragged board game and setting it down on the table. He blew dust off, and Abigail hastened to cover their mugs before a gray mass clouded both and made them undrinkable. "Sorry," he said sheepishly, and Abigail bit her tongue at yet another comparison of father and daughter. He grabbed the limp napkin and wiped off the top until the Game of Life logo was a smidge brighter to read.

"I guess mom did," she finally said. "I think there's a newer version now."

"Yeah, with credit cards so we don't have to count all the bills," Sawyer said. "I wonder how much it is? Think they have different car models?"

"No! I want to play this one." Celeste snatched the top off, nearly ripping the cardboard, and a new way of dust flew into the air. Coughing through it, she took out the spinner and the bent Career cards. "Oh, I want to be yellow!" She clutched the car and held it in the air before settling on the floor and driving it over the tile.

"I guess I know what we'll be doing when you leave," Abigail said as she handed Sawyer his coffee.

"What time is it?" he asked.

"Hmm, a quarter to 1. Why?"

Sawyer shrugged off his coat. "I think I have time for a quick game."

Celeste squealed and grabbed more of the game pieces. Sawyer grabbed the money bills before she could and carefully hid them on the windowsill where she couldn't reach.

"When has this game ever been quick?" Abigail asked although she sat back down anyway.

"It can be as quick or as long as we want," he said. He unfolded the game board and set the spinner in place to more squealing from Celeste as she spun it repeatedly. Sawyer and Abigail set up the rest of the game until Celeste grabbed another piece from the box.

"I want the green car!" she cried out. "Vroom!" She jumped to her feet and drove the plastic piece over every surface she could reach.

"I thought we lost the green car," Sawyer said. His eyebrows knitted together as Abigail raised hers.

"Maybe Mom found it. Besides, you've been the red car forever."

"Yeah, but green was my favorite color. You remember."

Abigail groaned and took a gulp of her too-hot coffee, ignoring the longing gaze Sawyer had on the red car in his daughter's hands as she drove it over the sofa.

Yearning

Why can't the warmth soothe my bones
The way it soothed yours?
Am I destined to know the love of the addict
Without tasting the desire of the addiction?
The blood coursing through my dying veins
Drips with languish and whiskey shots under neon lights.
Sunlight scorches less severely than the beer sign shimmering
Above your head when I see you behind my eyes.
I drink whiskey to recreate the scene,
But without director notes,
I meander into dive bars and dark alleyways,
Never reaching the illumination I depended on
When you'd light another cigarette between your teeth.
Drugs and alcohol are romanticized as the candy of gods,
But everyone looks away
When the yellowed eyes and brittle nails
Tarnish the gala decor, and the once shimmering dresses
And crisp black suits tremble and fade into watery hazes
As worn-out jeans and stained billiards shirts replace
Any facade of formal brilliance and marbled floors.
Is it wrong to wonder how it helped you?
Did it ever help, or was it merely keeping you on life support
Until you decided enough was enough
And took the doctor's medicine with a peaceful composure
On your weary face, my mother's hand within reach
And the television lighting the way?
I never feel soothed by the fire
On my tongue because you proved
That all the blazes in the world wouldn't be enough
When I found myself alone, looking at the early morning sky
The day you were finally called home.

Vow

I cannot understand the fight you face each day, hour, minute for months, years, decades, but I know you are deserving of love, help, forgiveness and that we, the sober and clean, may never possess the ability to give you everything we receive simply because we are not tethered to a substance.

May you find a person who can love you through your worst and your best and who can see the difference between your heart and your vice. May you never push away the person you love the most and may they always remember why they love you even as they hear of reasons to walk away. May your family and friends be there when you need them, whether you call on them seven times or seventy times seven.

Please be patient with us as we work through our fears, trauma, and esteem. We know you need help, but the more we give, the less we have, and the last thing we want to do is turn our backs on the one we love to preserve the love we have for ourselves. Always apologize and always promise to do better. Always resist the urge and always confide in us when you are safe to do so.

I have loved so many people in this life, and I have turned my back on so many. My love is endless, but my care is not. If I have left you in your darkest year, please forgive me but understand that another received the care they needed and lived to see the next morning. If you are still struggling, there are people who can help. They are here. They're here for *you*.

I vow to be the best version of myself to uplift your memory, your image, and all of you until the day the breath leaves my body. May you vow the same if only for yourself.

Kintsugi

Kintsugi pottery is an ancient Japanese practice
Of repairing broken pottery with gold
And creating a new work of art in the process.
I hope our memories will be as golden as the sun
And patch together these broken hearts
Into a masterpiece we couldn't see before.
Sometimes we can't repair what's broken
Because it was never meant to be.
We find new purpose in recreation,
And starting over is always clean,
Even if you've filled your cracks with so much gold
That you shine like the brilliant gem you are.
I wonder if you ever gave yourself clean slates,
Or if you held on to your chalky, dusty board
And punished yourself for mistakes we'd forgotten.
I pray your passing molded your pain in gold
Because your memory is the only thing
That keeps me from falling apart
When I think I can't take another day without you.

Onion-Flavored Memories

I vividly recall the nights I cried
And begged to be released from the screaming
And the tantrum-throwing guise
Of your worst night,
But they fade faster now that you're gone.
Instead of buying a bottle of whiskey
For your upcoming birthday,
We buy Reese's and Funyuns to share
And remember how the more processed the food,
The deeper your love for it.
I see new flavors of your favorite treats
And imagine how excited you'd be,
Driving to every grocery store and dollar store
In a fifteen-mile radius to find them.
The peak of these onion-flavored memories
And peanut butter scented reflections
Brings me back to your greatest traits
Instead of the worst ones we swept under the rug.

This One's for Dad

I'm sorry I could never find the words to speak
When you were still with me,
But I don't think they would have done this justice.
I wish I could have told you every word
Dashing across the page as I write,
But they would have caused more stress and pain
Than they could ever cause now
Because now I believe you understand me.
I keep your phone by my side of the bed
And I check on your truck in the driveway
To pretend as though you're here through these objects
And not energy coursing through the universe
Or living in Heaven with your family and friends.
I'm sorry I never spoke to you about my fears,
And I'm sorry our relationship was strained on both sides,
But I don't regret any of my decisions in the end
Because my only job was distracting you from the pain,
And I hope I did it okay even though we both know
You'd never show the truth to anyone but me and Mom.
You always wanted to be strong for others
When we only needed you to be strong for yourself.
Nothing can change how our lives played out,
But even the darkest nights are behind me.
I hope these words find you now, somehow,
Because they're for you,
And for all the ones who try to be their best.
That's all you can be, and that's what you were.

This is me letting go of the fears
I instilled in myself for survival.
This is an apology to my childhood,
A reflection of my adulthood,
A lesson from my lovers,
And a letter to my father.
I can't promise to be perfect,
But I promise to be me
And to be all you made me into.
Death will not separate us forever,
And life will never be the same,
But we spent time together in this space,
And I could never picture a more perfect place
Than the one I held by your side.

If you or someone you love needs help concerning substance abuse and/or addiction, there are resources and individuals available to you.

Alcoholics Anonymous

www.aa.org

There are dozens of local chapters available throughout the United States, and all are welcome to sit in and hear from those who are actively working on overcoming their abuse or addiction. I highly recommend sitting in on at least one meeting for those married to, friends with, or who are the child of an addict to better understand the crippling dependence they have on their substance.

National Institute on Alcohol Abuse and Alcoholism

https://www.niaaa.nih.gov/publications/brochures-and-fact-sheets/treatment-alcohol-problems-finding-and-getting-help

Crisis Text Line

Text HOME to 741741 to reach a trained Crisis Counselor

SAMHSA's National Helpline

1-800-662-HELP (4357)

Thank you for reading! If you enjoyed this collection, please consider leaving a review on Amazon and Goodreads as it really helps other readers find my books.

You're not alone.
It's not your fault.

No matter what decision you made to help them or yourself, I'm so proud of you.

About the Author

Amber Campbell is a jack-of-all-trades in the writing world: she's worked in writing, editing, and agenting (as an intern but she won't stop talking about it) before learning publishing and marketing for her poetry collections.

When she's not meticulously weaving words into sentences, she can be found in her tiny home in Texas with her husband, fur babies, and semi-aquatic son (Golden Thread Turtle).

You can find her online @AmberCampbellBooks.

www.ingramcontent.com/pod-product-compliance
Lightning Source LLC
Chambersburg PA
CBHW051446140726

47987CB00006B/2570